WRITE TO PUBLISH

TOM BIRD

SOJOURN PUBLISHING, LLC
SEDONA, AZ

Write to Publish

For permissions:

Sojourn Publishing, LLC, 280 Foothills South Dr., Sedona, AZ 86336

ISBN-13: 978-1-62747-013-1 (paperback)
ISBN-13: 978-1-62747-014-8 (ebook)

Printed in the United States of America

Contents

Introduction

For the first time in history, the opportunity exists to not only become the published author of a book, but much more importantly, to rise, and rise rapidly, to the ranks of being a best-selling author without selling your soul.

I know Borders has closed and Barnes & Noble is preparing for either a major sell-off or bankruptcy. Even though those moves may comprise a major personal tragedy of sorts for employees of those two corporations, for us, as authors, they signal a major breakthrough—one which, if taken advantage of, can lead you to the type of personal, professional, and financial fame as an author you could only have dreamt of before.

Read on…

Tom Bird

Chapter One
Take a Long Exhale

I have been working with aspiring authors for the last three decades. One of my most unique and identifiable strengths is that I focus a great deal of my efforts on dealing with who the authors are on the inside, on what makes them tick.

It's simply not enough to offer a proven, successful method to writing or publishing a book if the user is unable to implement it due to past experiences that resulted in personal baggage.

With that in mind, it's time to get rid of that unnecessary baggage and inappropriate thinking that has held you down for so long. For your literary heaven awaits! To get there, to embrace the blessed opportunities which are now presenting themselves to all authors, we must go beyond the confusions, angers, and misguided directions of the past. We must rise above them to reach our own personal heavens. The route to that blessed of all places is easy to find and comfortable to ride, but first you have to go there. For as long as it has been reaching out to you, like all of us, you have innocently and blindly moved away from it. Now it's time to go home!

In that light, let's take a deep breath together, followed by an even deeper exhale. Do that right now.

Breath is an amazing thing. Through doing it consciously we can accomplish much, and more rapidly and thoroughly than through other more tedious and expensive methods.

Breathing is the essence of life, of your true self, and exhaling all of the unnecessary personal residue is the quickest and easiest way to let that which you no longer need leave your body, soul, and mind, allowing you to elevate back to the home from which we all came.

Especially keep in mind that it's the exhale that releases the tension, the residue of past mistakes. The deeper the exhale, the more tension is released.

Take another deep breath and a clearer exhale. Get used to doing that as you move through this book. Sure, things are changing and that change is drastic and painful for so many, but the change is not only necessary—it is good—especially for you. Know that you will end up in a better place on the other side of these changes. You will end up where you are meant to be: back to your true home, the place of acceptance, love, and brilliance from which we all emerge.

Inhale—that's it—and exhale deeply. Blow out any resistance you may be feeling. Let that stuff from your past go: your past thinking, the pain associated with past failures in writing and/or publishing, and any anger or frustration you may have as a result of those failures. Throw a pillow against the wall if you have to, cry, scream, whatever. Just let all that you no longer need, and which does not serve you, to be released. It hasn't served you and isn't serving you now. In fact, it's eating up all of the space that you will desperately need for the information you are about to absorb.

This new system is vastly different from what we knew before. It will not only be a lot better but vastly more efficient—much faster, easier, more successful, and for you as an author, more profitable—even as a new author—by a minimum of 800 percent.

Are you feeling any better? Has the necessary room been cleared in your mind for the reality and brilliance of now?

If not, exhale deeply—this time so deeply that your diaphragm comes way in and your shoulders round to meet it.

Exhale. It has been said that when God closes a door, he also opens a window.

In this case, he has closed a door and opened a garage door for a four-car garage, and you—yes, you, right now—will be the recipient of that opening.

Exhale.

Hallelujah!

Now, before going on to the next chapter, go to my

website, *www.TomBird.com*, click on the icon entitled "FREEBIES," download my free *Transitioning Back to the Author You Were Meant to Be* CD.

Begin starting your day by first listening to the six-minute relaxation Track One of the CD. Then let it roll over to Track Two and play that side in the background as often as possible as you move through your day.

Track Two is subliminal, so you can play it while you're doing just about anything. Initially, there is nothing better for helping you reprogram yourself and your life for the success that awaits you than breathing properly and listening to Track Two of this CD. More than anything else, when these two actions are used in conjunction with each other, they will become responsible for charting the route back to your real self, and the success you deserve as an author.

Chapter Two
The Way Things Used to Be

Even though it desperately needs to be addressed, I am not going to spend a whole lot of time on the following material because doing so could be seen as negative. There's just no way that could benefit us here in the present, on the far side, away from the past.

Here's how the book publishing industry, which I will hereto reference as "conventional publishing," has worked and still, as it is hanging on by its fingernails, attempts to work. The best way that I can think of describing it in general is through the following analogy.

Once while in Virginia Beach, I was meeting a few dozen friends out for dinner. When it came time for dessert, I ordered something completely decadent. Since there were so many of us crammed into a tight space, it was just easier for our server to hand the dessert to someone on the opposite side of the table and request for it to be passed to me. As the desert was passed down, each person that handled it took a bite. When it finally arrived to me, almost all of the decadent aspects were gone, and there was one lone, tiny bite left.

That's the way conventional publishing has worked with its authors for the last several hundred years. Considering the alternatives that currently exist, I no longer recommend it as a front line for publishing a book.

Here's a bit more about how conventional book publishing works.

- You create and pay for the product, in this case your book, just like I worked for the money to pay for my dessert.

- However, after everyone in the industry, from your publishing house to distributors and/or bookstores, takes their cut of your work, you end up having given away 90 percent of the profitable enjoyability of your book. For example, if your book sells for $20, you will be lucky to make 10 percent of that, or $2. Some publishing houses even take a greater cut of your work.

One author I am working for paid a conventional publisher to publish his book. For every book that sells he makes eighty-nine cents. Another author of mine spent $105,000 to get three of her books published with iUniverse, a paid publisher. Over the next eighteen months she earned less than $50 in royalties on her $105,000 investment. Where did all of the money go that she could have earned on her book? Certainly not to her! Just like my dessert analogy, by the time the profits trickled down to her, they were almost all gone.

This won't happen to you, of course, because you're reading this book and you're going to put into play what it has to say. However, the facts and figures from above do give credence to the old adage that authors do not make money.

On one level I agree with that statement. But, to make it completely true from my perspective, I would have to modify that slightly to say, "Uninformed authors don't make money."

Publishing through what is still left of conventional publishing, what is the best-case scenario you can make off of 100,000 sales of your book, if each sale grossed a profit of $20?

The reason I chose 100,000 copies sold in my explanation is because selling 100,000 copies would land you on just about every worthy bestseller list around, which becomes important down the line.

Okay, back to the answer you are waiting for.

The best case financial scenario you could expect to experience on selling 100,000 copies of your book through a conventional publisher would be a $200,000 profit.

Now, even though that may or may not sound like a lot of money to you, let's put that in perspective.

Being a bestseller means that you have reached the top of your profession. If you were at the top of your profession in acting or directing, you could expect to make tens of millions of dollars per movie. The same is true with sports, another entertainment field. Why, then, would you not be as highly regarded as an author? Because 90 percent of your profit is eaten away—remember my dessert analogy—and thus, you never see or enjoy the success.

So, if your book sold for $20 and you received 100 percent of the profit on the same 100,000 copies, you would make two million dollars, which would be comparable to what other entertainers would receive.

Do you see what I am getting at? Would you really be able to take in that type of revenue from your book? The answer to your question is yes. Read on.

Before we move into the glorious facts and figures that you want to hear more about, it is essential that you become acquainted with the potential pitfalls that await you out there on the road to successful self-publishing, so you don't innocently fall into any of them.

Chapter Three
The Royalty Myth

For centuries authors have amassed their incomes through the acquisition of royalties.

Royalties offer you a percentage of either gross or net profits derived from a book. In today's world, receiving a 10-percent royalty rate from the cover price of a book, like the analogy that I used previously, would be considered generous.

However, I want to stress that even though you put the time and energy into producing the product—your book—it was the publishers who put up the hard cash to publish and sell it, which is how they justify the tiny royalty rate they offer authors. For this reason, the basic concept of royalties was seen as "fair" from a business perspective.

Of course, the aversion by many authors, including the legendary Stephen King, to the tiny percentage received has been well documented. In comparison to most other business models their anger is well justified. Yet, it is enough for us to know right now that the publishers collected the more sizable percentage of the profits because they completely shouldered the financial risk associated with the production, publication, distribution, and sale of a book.

What would happen if you, yourself, shouldered that burden? What if you wrote and produced the product, paid for any editing, production costs, and promotion? Should whomever you pay for these services—those who have been paid in full and profited from your payment for their services—be given a percentage of the eventual profits from the sale of your book, even though they in no way contributed anything to the book outside of the work for which they were already compensated?

If you said anything other than no, you need to have your head examined. As unfair as this would be to you, if that were the case—just as it was the case with the two authors whose stories I shared in the last chapter. And that is what today's publishers are asking of authors!

So, let's detail how that works. Here's the entire scenario.

- You write the book; you produce the product.

- You pay for the editing, production, publication, and promotion of the book.

- Then when the book sells, you earn 25 percent of the revenue from each sale, which is much higher than normally earned by a first-time author aligned with a conventional publisher—the hook used by these companies.

What that translates into is you making absolutely no money, or even losing money, on a book sale. Let me show you how that works. Here's the entire scenario.

1. Your book sells for, let's say, $20.

2. You receive a royalty rate of 25 percent off the cover price of the book. So you receive $5. (Okay, that sounds a lot better than $2.)

3. However, since you are shouldering the entire financial burden for the production and publication of the book, you have hard costs to deduct. Let's say the book costs $3.50 to produce and $1.50 to ship to the buyer, which you are responsible for paying. There goes your $5, leaving you with a profit of $0. Where does the other $15 go? Into the pocket of the company you had already compensated in advance for their services and from which they had already derived a profit.

So, in moving forward, what do you need to do to avoid falling into this burning cauldron of disappointment?

Avoid entering into a partnership with any entity that would expect any upfront money from you of any amount, and that limits your profit margin from that derived by royalties.

Why? If you are shouldering 100 percent of the costs associated with writing the book and 100 percent of the financial burden associated with production of the book, you should receive what percentage of the profits?

Correct: 100 percent.

Nothing less is acceptable, and if you want to be the successful, wealthy author that today's New Age of Publishing offers you the opportunity to be, you are going to have to fall in line with the already established system that exists for you to do just that.

One hundred percent of the profits is what you will need to expect—and nothing less!

Chapter Four
Direct or Indirect

In today's book-publishing world, the opportunity exists for many alternatives that were not available to authors in the past, including direct marketing to the consumer. You see, that's where conventional publishers hamstrung authors in the past. In essence, they had a monopoly on how and to whom a book would be published because they controlled, at least indirectly, the bookstores. The bookstores, in response, normally only displayed books on their shelves that were published by houses they recognized. That is why conventional book publishers got away with charging you a 90-percent profit margin for the publication of your book and the representation of it to bookstores. For, without them, you would have had a difficult, if not impossible time trying to get your book in bookstores.

However, with bookstores going down and

opportunities available through the internet rising, you can now get directly to the book buyer, so your larger profits are no longer held hostage by a conventional publisher.

What this all translates to is that you can be your own publisher! Just hire a fulfillment house to fulfill your orders and easily take home $16 on the same $20 book.

So, if you sold 100,000 copies of your book at a clear profit of $16 per sale, you would make $1.6 million. Sounds a lot better than the $200,000 you would have made going through a conventional publisher, doesn't it?

The key to receiving this type of profit margin is tied to your ability to sell directly to a consumer. Using direct marketing, a consumer buys your book through you, your website, or whatever venue is personally linked to you. Again, a good fulfillment house or just and autoresponder system tied to sales from your website can manage this part of the process. So, no worries. More on this later.

Indirect sales, which do become a necessity to really saturate your publishing efforts for your audience, are when you sell your book through a sales site. Bookstores—including online bookstores—are nothing more than indirect sales sites.

For indirect sales, the amount of profit required to be shared by you will be between 5 and 50 percent. So, of course, you want to focus as much time and energy as possible on direct-sales opportunities, especially to make the high-end percentages listed above.

You can avoid this entire percentage altogether, as any internet marketer will tell you, through the proper sales strategy and approach, which is where the real profits can be made.

Chapter Five: The Self-Publishing Myth And Potential

For centuries, self-publishing a book has been likened to taking your sister to the prom because you weren't able to get another date.

Nothing could be further from the truth.

Gee, I wonder who was spreading these rumors? I am sure that it couldn't have been those guys that were deriving 90 percent of authors' profits for literally doing nothing. Nah, not those guys. They and the monopoly they created, along with their plan to extort money from unsuspecting authors, were always looking out for the best interest of authors. Sure.

In reality, the world's finest authors have used self-publishing to eventually reach the level of prominence that they deserved.

Do you recognize any of these names?

- Mark Twain
- Walt Whitman
- Henry David Thoreau
- John Grisham

This represents just a partial list of self-publishing authors. I just didn't want to bore you with a list that could go on and on. I think you got my point.

How could this be? How could the professionally trained eyes of those in conventional book publishing actually miss such brilliance?

For an in-depth understanding of how this happened, I would suggest picking up a copy of Elaine Borish's *Unpublishable!* which only costs $12.95—and is worth every penny.

Here's the reality behind how such a travesty as the one I am referring to took place.

- The publishing industry, like any other investment business, is made up of trend followers.
- Trend followers would prefer to safely invest their funds in products that have an already proven track record.
- Here's where the conflict comes in. Bestselling

authors are normally trendsetters.

- This causes a natural conflict between them and the trend followers in book publishing.

- This eventually propels the soon-to-be finest, earthshaking, bestselling authors of any generation to be rejected, leading them toward self-publishing.

Chapter Six: Former Drawbacks of Self-Publishing

Before the technological breakthroughs of the mid-1990s, self-publishing had some significant drawbacks.

First, it was very expensive, primarily because your book had to be typeset by hand. That would usually cost tens of thousands of dollars.

Second, authors had to order a large quantity of books per print run because of the high price of printing; starting up the press; hiring employees to present, ink, paper, and power the press in order to spread out the initial expense of producing their book over as many volumes as possible. This was the only way the cost-per-item price could drop down low enough to make a few dollars per book.

Third, this process cost the author tens of thousands

of dollars to produce an inventory of books that he or she would never be able to get rid of because of the stranglehold kept on bookstores by conventional publishers. This stranglehold prohibited “outside” books from being hosted in bookstores because they had not been published by an affiliate of one of the bookstores.

Chapter Seven
Self-Publishing Today

Self-publishing today couldn't be any more different than the self-publishing of the mid-1990s. How?

1. You can get your book formatted, which is the modern version of typesetting, for a fraction of the price it used to cost. In fact, you can get a book formatted, published, and distributed internationally by the top distributor of books in the world for a few thousand dollars. What that usually translates to is having to sell less than 300 books to clear your initial investment, after which you will be taking home 100 percent of the net sales from the book.

2. You can get your book formatted, published,

and distributed worldwide in as little as a few weeks, enabling you to take advantage of any current media trends—and these trends are essential to the sale of a book. This is a huge plus because one of the major drawbacks with conventional publishing is that it takes so long to get a book onto the shelves. Any trends that could aid in the sale of a book usually expire by the time a book is actually released. This super-slow turnaround time also leaves conventional publishers literally taking wild guesses at what books would be selling a few years down the road, which was obviously impossible to do in the past and even more improbable in today's faster moving world.

3. Today's self-publishing offers you direct access to readers. You no longer have to go through bookstores that you have to hope and pray will not only carry your book but represent it properly.

4. Today's self-publishing offers complete creative, editorial, and promotional freedom to the author. In the past, writers had to accept whatever advice was offered in these areas. Today, however, authors can form their own creative, editorial, and promotional teams around them, choosing from the best the industry has to offer. These experts are now generally available to

assist you at very reasonable prices after having been let go by the conventional publishing houses where they used to work.

In summary, the self-publishing world of today offers an author complete creative, editorial, and promotional freedom, a profit margin unheard of before, and the opportunity to get a book that is professionally published and distributed worldwide in a matter of days, enabling you to go from the author you always wanted to be to a published author.

Is this your dream—but you haven't written your book yet?

If so, check out my website, *www.WriteYourPublishable-BookInAWeekend.com*, and my book titled ***YOU CAN... WRITE YOUR BOOK IN A WEEKEND.***

Chapter Eight
Market Value

MARKET VALUE EQUATES TO WHAT YOU ARE worth, especially in the world of book publishing.

Now, here's the good news: a high-ranking market value is at your disposal, and it's not very far off at that! First, let's discuss what market value is and what it means to an author.

Market value, often referred to as a platform in the world of conventional publishing, is nothing more than name recognition and credential or presence appreciation.

Market value for an author used to be directly tied to whether or not a conventional publisher published your book. If someone didn't publish your book, you were looked down upon by those who would have normally tried to sell your book, such as bookstore owners and managers.

Today, market value equates to what you have accomplished and how many people recognize you as a result.

For example, market value can be defined by how many people recognize your name in your town or your chosen profession—all the way down to how many friends you have on Facebook, or how many people follow you on Twitter, or how many people you have access to through email lists. Market value is a dilemma faced by every new author; you land sales as the result of your name recognition, but you don't receive name recognition without selling your book.

So the fastest, best, and easiest way to acquire market value or name recognition comes through book sales.

In the past, when conventional publishing dominated the book-publishing market, value for a new author could be acquired through competition. For example, the more literary agents who were interested in representing your book to publishers, or the higher the ranking of the literary agents who were interested in presenting you, the more market value you had in the eyes of publishers. In fact, as the result of having one high-powered agent representing a book or dozens interested in representing it, I have seen new authors go from being unpublished to on the top of a conventional publisher's list of their best authors.

In this, the New Age of Publishing, during which time the influence of conventional publishers has been de-emphasized, market value equates to sales.

So, how do you get those sales and acquire the necessary market value? Read on…

Chapter Nine
What Makes a Book Sell?

First of all, before I go further, let me clarify for you that promotion can bring attention to the existence of a book, but it cannot sell the book. Read that statement again, this time out loud and release a big exhale while doing so.

Yes, what I am saying is that if a book is good enough it will sell; if it's not, it won't. So, what makes a book sell?

There are several factors: for example, topic and timeliness. However, the main factors that determine whether a book sells are author's voice, style, depth, personality, and heartfelt approach.

In other words, nobody writes shallow books that become successful anymore. Information isn't enough. Today's readers are too picky for that to happen. The bottom line is that they want to be entertained while being informed. Their lives are just too short to be wasted on reading something that doesn't touch them deeply while doing so.

So, how do you entertain a reader? Does it mean that you have to make them laugh each time they pick up your book?

That would help, but making them laugh is not an absolute necessity. However, making them *feel* is. So, if you make them cry, laugh, smile—if you deeply move them in some way—you have succeeded. If you haven't, you've failed. It's that simple.

How do you make them feel an emotion? By feeling that emotion yourself first.

How do you do that?

If you haven't already done so, I would suggest ready my book, *You Can... Write Your Book in a Weekend*, and it will tell you, in great depth, how to do just that.

So, let's say that you've already written a moving book or are planning on writing one, what do you do then to acquire market value?

Simple. You saturation publish.

Saturation publishing is exclusive to the New Age of Publishing. It is taking advantage of every route possible to get to every one of your potential readers no matter what their areas of interest.

For example, in today's publishing world there are those people who prefer to take advantage of the latest trend by reading their books as ebooks on Kindle, iPads, Nooks, or their Sony E-readers. There will be some readers who prefer audio books. Others prefer books published by print-on-demand services, which for years now have offered authors a much greater degree of creative and expressive freedom.

Then, of course, there are those who have stuck to their guns, refused to change, and will only read books that are credibly published, as they see it, by conventional publishers.

The last group of readers are a dying breed. In fact, in July 2010 the *Wall Street Journal* reported that for the first time in publishing history, ebooks outsold hard copy books published by conventional publishers during the previous month. This trend continues to skyrocket, with more and more readers moving over to the convenient and more ecologically sound option of ebooks every day.

So popular has this trend become that at present, potential customers entering Barnes & Noble are immediately met by a sales representative trying to sell them a Nook, their version of an ebook reader. In reality, Barnes & Noble and other chains have become so desperate to keep up with the move to ebooks that they are willing to sacrifice potential sales of hard-copy books in their stores by pushing their Nook on customers as soon as they walk through the door.

Chapter Ten
How Saturation Publishing Works

Again, saturation publishing is taking advantage of the ability to meet all potential readers of your book where they are and through whichever platform they choose to read.

This form of product saturation was not easily accessible in the past because of the monopoly conventional publishers had over readers worldwide. They chose how and when a book would be published, with most decisions designed to meet their own needs more than that of the books they were representing—or the authors who had written them.

However, now with that industry crumbling to its knees, and the combination of the miraculous technological advancements that have transpired as of late—supported by consumers—authors can now have full control over the sales destiny of their books.

This is the case because:

1. Popular, acceptable inroads have been created for them to connect directly with the consumer. No longer do they have to go through a series of middle men who not only feed off the vast majority of an author's potential profit, but in general, interfere with the flow of how books can best be represented and delivered to the consumer.

2. The strategies and applications for directly reaching and approaching readers are now available to everyone.

3. The cost of preparing a book for publication and getting it published, which generally runs less than half of the cost of a semester's tuition at an average state university or college, is affordable for most.

4. A book can now be moved through the phases of writing, editing, and publication quickly, oftentimes in a few weeks, to enable an author to be able to take full advantage of a sales trend or opportunity, thus greatly increasing the book's chance of being a financial success. This can create an almost instant, overnight name recognition and potential career for a would-be author.

5. Authors currently have four easily accessible options through which to publish their books, offering the opportunity to get their works out quickly and directly into the hands of the consumers who purchase cross-media products.

6. If publication of an author's work in any one of these four venues achieves success, that success will immediately spread its influence in the direction of the other three areas, resulting in what appears to be instant literary stardom for the author.

7. In the past, authors were offered only one alternative for success and that was through the route of conventional publishing.

8. However, several factors significantly deflated an author's opportunity for success, let alone what could appear as instant success.

9. The major components that robbed authors of this opportunity were:

    - a slow turnaround in the publishing process of the conventional publisher, which curtailed an author's ability to take full advantage of a trend before it expired;

    - a lack of personal creative, expressive, and

promotional control over a book, thereby keeping an author from more effectively reaching readers;

- a shortage of publishing options to effectively reach the entirety of an author's full readership.

Chapter Eleven
Much More on The Individual Components of Saturation Publishing

As I mentioned before, there are currently four options available for the publication and circulation of a book, which are defined and discussed below.

To fully take advantage of the opportunities that are available for the eventual publishing success of your book, I strongly suggest moving into all four areas at the same time.

Again, when one area hits and sales start to blossom, that influence will quickly spread to the other directions, offering you the opportunity to potentially become an overnight success.

Ebooks.

In reality, an ebook is nothing more than a universally accepted text file. That's all.

As a result, you can literally create one within an hour—at no cost—simply by going to *www.adobe.com.*

The folks at Adobe allow you to create a few PDF files, another version of a universally accepted text file, for free. Simply upload your Word document, or any other version of a word processing file you use, into their system, ask it to transform it into a PDF file (this will usually take less than an hour), and you are ready to go with your ebook.

However, there is a major drawback to this simple system of publication: readers worldwide have become so savvy that they don't want to just read a book; they want the ebooks they choose to read to actually look like books.

That's where formatting, which is the modern-day computerized version of typesetting, comes in. To offer your readership what they really want and what they have become accustomed to, you will need to have your book formatted.

And yes, you can format your book yourself. However, the software you will need is costly, often running upwards of a thousand dollars; the learning curve to master using it is steep, often taking several months; and unless you are extremely great with the program you choose to use, the end result comes out looking unprofessional. No matter how well written a book is, if it looks bad it usually doesn't attract readers.

What is the price of having a book formatted by a high-level, professional formatter?

Depending upon the length of your book, it will usually run at approximately the same cost as the software you would need in order to do your own formatting.

One thing to keep in mind is the importance of having your book formatted for use with the latest ebook readers: iPad and Kindle, for example. They each call for a special ebook format for a book to be able to run on their system.

How long does it take to get a book formatted?

Depending upon the schedule of the formatter, a regular order can usually be completed in a week to ten days. Rush orders, which are much more expensive, can usually be turned around in a few days.

Now, let's turn to editing. Before we go further, here is what I want to share with you on editing: get your book professionally edited before having it published. Better yet, have any and all editing done before you take your work to the formatter; otherwise, you will end up having to pay your formatter extra for redoing the book after any editorial comments or changes are taken into account.

What type of editing needs to be done?

Before I answer that question, let me state clearly that taking responsibility for editing of your manuscript is just an assumed responsibility that comes along with the New Age of Book Publishing.

Yes, you have to bare the expense. That's the bad news.

But the good news is that in the economy of today's self-publishing market, you can choose your own editor and build your own handpicked editorial team. Your editorial team can fit your specific needs. They will greatly increase the quality of your efforts and the quality of your execution.

This is what will eventually lead to the sale of your book. And you can do this for much less cost than you could years ago.

Lastly, you can hire the finest personnel in the world to go to work on your book, especially now that the conventional publishers have let go of so many of the top editorial minds in the industry.

That said, with all of those great editorial options available to you, don't hire anyone less than the best for your book if giving your book the best chance to sell is what you really want to do.

Sure, you can get a friend to give it a quick read for a cheap price, or maybe you know a retired English teacher who could use a few bucks. However, the difference between your buddy or your friend, the retired English teacher, and a top-notch editor is huge.

Don't cut corners. Go the whole way. Give your book the absolute best chance to succeed. Find and hire a top-notch editor.

What type of editing do you need? You need two forms: style editing and copy editing.

Style editing comes in the form of a manuscript evaluation. This is when you submit your manuscript, along with a general information sheet, which covers what your intentions are, with your book, to a proven style editor. This professional then reviews your manuscript on the basis of style, general execution, and how well you meet the needs of your proposed audience.

A written review of your manuscript is normally prepared and sent to you.

Being able to connect with the style editor in regard to his/her suggestions is normally an option as well, and the price is usually included in the price that was paid for the review.

Once your book has been style edited and all of the necessary changes needing to be made are completed, your book should be transferred to a copy editor.

As with the style editor, be sure to get a proven copy editor to review your book. I suggest this even in the case where you feel your grammar and spelling skills are top-notch because no matter how good an author may be in this essential area, we can all grow blind in regard to our own work. You don't want to get caught with your pants down.

Once these essential edits have been completed and all of the necessary changes have been made, your book then goes to your formatter, who will design the cover and contents of your book. Be sure to clarify in advance how the cover of your book will be handled.

Print-on-Demand (POD) Books

POD books are hard copy versions of your book that are formatted, published and promoted by you. POD books typically possess (if done correctly) the same quality as a book published by a conventional publisher. In fact, conventional publishing methods of professional print publishing are available to you as the author of a POD book.

The big difference, of course, is that by not using conventional publishers to provide this service, you are prohibiting them from siphoning off 90 percent of your potential revenue. Thus, instead of receiving $2 from the sale of a $20 book, after your own production and fulfillment costs, you will instead garner around $15 per sale on a book that is selling for $20.

The entire concept surrounding POD books was spearheaded by Ingram, the largest, most respected distributor of books in the world. (By the way, a book distributor, by definition, is a warehousing entity that purchases books from publishers at a quantity discount and then resells those books to stores and other retailers for a smaller discount off the cover price of the book; this is where they derive their profit.)

Ingram, who has done this better than anyone in the history of book publishing, came up with the idea for POD in the mid-1990s.

Their idea revolved around the uploading of properly formatted books by authors to their POD subsidiary, Lightning Source Press. Once books were received, they charged the author a small fee and they were entered into Ingram's computerized distribution system. That way, whenever a book was purchased or ordered by a reader it could be immediately printed in-house, by Lightning Source (LS), and sent to the customer.

LS's computerized system of being able to literally print a book on demand, as opposed to the outdated method of only being able to run off books en masse, offers authors the opportunity to save tens of thousands of dollars per book, making the publication of one's own book affordable to a much greater number of writers.

With the POD system, LS only prints a book when there is a paid demand for it—very efficient, economical, and author-friendly.

Since LS literally returns 100 percent of the profit from a book to the author, as opposed to ripping the author off through false royalties, they are the only POD company I recommend. In addition, the fact that they are a subsidiary of Ingram doesn't hurt either.

To submit your book to them, you will need to have it properly formatted and readied for publication. You will also need to fill out some paperwork for them and pay them a small fee. For more information on Lightning Source, visit their website at *www.lightningsource.com.*

Regarding the formatting of your POD book, the process is very similar to that of ebooks. So, once you have hired a seasoned, professional formatter, he or she should be able to format both your POD book and ebook.

Audio Books

In the past, the consumption of audio books was normally limited to traveling salespeople and those who were visually impaired.

However, with the computer age and the popularity of iTunes and other similar programs, audio books have become more prevalent. Audio books read personally by the author, which serves to bridge the gap between reader and writer, are becoming especially popular.

To become an audio book author, all you need is either a computerized recording system—there are several high-quality and inexpensive options available—or a recording studio, and you are all set to go.

With the cyber world creating greater and greater personal distance between us, readers crave any form of closeness that brings them a more intimate experience with the authors who most influence their lives. Thus, they don't care if one of their favorite authors makes a mistake or two in the reading of his or her book; what readers crave most is any form of communication that offers them a bridge between themselves and an author. And audio books do just that.

Once the recording of your book is complete, sites such as iTunes and others make it relatively easy to upload your book to their sites for distribution, and presently they take only a tiny percentage of your profit for any sales.

Conventional Publishers

Conventional publishers may be on their way out, but they're not dead yet. There is still a very significant audience of readers worldwide who strongly prefer to purchase a hard copy of a book published by a convention publisher, directly from a bookstore.

As long as persons who feel that way are still around, we will always have physical bookstores. There is certainly nothing wrong with that. So many of us have enjoyed, for so long, not only hard copy versions of books, but also bookstores.

However, to significantly increase your chances of reaping a large sale and amount of money through the sale of a conventional book, as an author, you have to get a conventional house to commit as much money as possible to you upfront. That way you will be putting them in a position where they have to fight, through the accruing of a lot of sales from your book, to get their money back. Then and only then can you guarantee they will do a good job in both publishing and promoting your book.

How do you do that?

Two ways.

You can either create market value for yourself in their eyes through the sales of one of the above three options, or you can create pressure on them to purchase your book for a high price through competition to acquire the rights the book.

In regard to the second option, you can learn

everything you need to know about that in my book, *You Were Born to Publish*. To receive a free copy, simply drop me an email at *TomBird@TomBird.com*, with the above book title in the subject line, and I will email you a copy. Regarding the self-published versions of your book, check out the chapter on promotion that comes later in this book.

Other Technical Considerations If You Are Not Going the Conventional Route

To follow this divine route of publishing I am referring to as the New Age of Book Publishing, you will also need to take a few more things into consideration. Taking care of these is just the price you have to pay to offer yourself the greater creative and editorial expression and promotional control that are essential to the successful sale of your book. This will also provide you the opportunity to increase the profit margin of your book by an average of 800 percent.

Of course, none of these considerations is available if you go the conventional publishing route.

Even though the items discussed below may seem like a lengthy list of chores on which to follow through, in almost all cases, these are one-time tasks. Do them now and they are in place for each book you choose to publish from this point forward. By making the extra effort just once, they will serve you forever!

- **Website**—You will need to set up a website through which information on you can be found and direct sales of your book can be made.

- **Domain Name**—Make sure you secure the domain name for your site or else you may end up paying thousands of dollars for it later. I recommend going through GoDaddy for this service.

- **Hosting**—You will also need to enter into an agreement to have your site hosted on the Internet. I recommend GoDaddy for this service as well.

- **Shopping Cart**—This is an add-on to your website that will enable you to receive sales from consumers; the revenue you receive will go directly into your bank account. For this service, I recommend OneShoppingCart.

- **Bank Account**—You will need to set up a separate account to link to your shopping cart.

- **ISBN**—You will need a separate ISBN number, which is like a social security number, for each version of your book. I would recommend going through Bowker to acquire these.

- **Copyright**—Your book will need to be copyrighted after it is complete. Contact the Library of Congress to do so.

- **Trademark**—If you choose, you can trademark the title of your book as well. Doing so will protect it from being used by anyone else. I recommend going through either *legalzoom.com* or directly through the United States Patent & Trademark office.

- **Lightning Source**—Don't forget to review and then enter into your agreement with LS to have them produce and distribute your POD book.

Chapter Twelve
How Much Can You Really Make?

THAT'S THE BIG QUESTION THAT EVERYONE WANTS TO know, isn't it? How much can I really make from the sale of my book?

Let me answer that through sharing with you a potential scenario based on some facts and figures that I alluded to earlier.

Let's say the hard copy version of your timely book sells for $20, and after paying for the printing and shipping through LS, you make $15 per book sale through direct sales, and you sell 100,000 copies. That comes out to $1.5 million on the sale of the POD version of your book.

Then, based on the sale of that version going so well, you sell another 100,000 ebooks at $10 each—which is a good price for an ebook—through direct sales. You accrue another million dollars.

Your audio book version then takes off and sells well too, netting you another 100,000 sales at, after iTunes takes its commission, $6 each. That's another $600,000 you just made.

Now, with the sales of your book taking off this way, conventional publishers, having done their due diligence, will want to sell your book, too. Since your book has already sold so well on its own, there's a bidding war for the rights to it, and the price to acquire it jumps up to $1.5 million, which would not be unusual for a sale of this type.

With the speed of technology, all of this could transpire in a few short months. You could go from being a would-be author to a bestselling, world-renowned author, a millionaire author who made $4.6 million on the sale of his or her first book over just a few months, on an initial investment of only $6,000 to produce the book, for which you were completely reimbursed after only 400 sales of the POD version of your book.

Sound too good to be true?

It's not! Don't let your past attitude toward your real value to both yourself and the world get in the way of your success.

My buddy, Chris Guerrerio, has become one of the world's top internet marketing experts. He sold his first book, *Maximized Metabolism*, on the internet as an ebook with absolutely no experience in doing so.

In the first month alone he sold 60,000 copies at $10 each. Eventually, he went on to sell over a million copies at that price in just over eighteen months. You can do it, too! To check out more success stories like Chris's, visit my website, *www.tombird.com*.

Chapter Thirteen
The Fast, Efficient, Easy Way Out

A few years ago, I received a handwritten letter in the mail from a student of mine who had experienced great results using my system. I could tell by the flamboyant style of the handwriting that he was in a very inspired state when he wrote it. In the letter he challenged me to create a system for the rapid and efficient publication of books, one that would match the efficiency and precision of my Write Your Publishable Book in a Weekend Retreats. In doing so, as he said, budding authors could come to one of my retreats and not only write a book in record time, but get it published almost immediately afterward as well. And so the quest began.

I threw myself into studying the market and found some systems in place that did exactly what my student was encouraging me to do, but over the course of months as opposed to weeks, and cost a whopping $65,000. I also discovered a lot people who I would label as crooks. These individuals preyed on a new author's desperation, eventually taking advantage of them through the concept of what I refer to as "false royalties," which I covered earlier in the book.

Finally, after much studying, dozens of interviews, a lot of planning—and even more trial and error—I created a system for authors to get everything they needed to successfully complete and publish their books for up to one-twentieth of the price tag listed above.

To find out more about the Publish Now Program, you can either visit my website at *www.TomBird.com,* drop me a line at *TomBird@TomBird.com*, or call my office at 928-203-0265 and I will send you some in-depth material on the program.

Where do you go from here, budding author?

Anywhere you want! The world is yours for the taking, it is your jewel, and now you set the ship under your feet to sail that sea.

I wish you the best of luck on this marvelous and potentially highly profitable adventure. May you enjoy your life as an author with your newfound knowledge, which can now evolve into experience, excellence, and expertise!

www.ingramcontent.com/pod-product-compliance
Lightning Source LLC
LaVergne TN
LVHW050946080826
845145LV00004B/1422

* 9 7 8 1 6 2 7 4 7 0 1 3 1 *